Caleb's Colt

By
Jill Briscoe

Illustrated by
Russ Flint

Ideals Publishing Corporation
Nashville, Tennessee

ISBN 0-8249-8112-X

THE SUN HAD JUST COME UP
when Caleb clattered into the courtyard to join his father.

"I want to go with you today,"
Caleb said.

His father smiled. Today they
were to go and see the colt who had
been tied up to a donkey stake in the
long grass. It was time to move the
animal so he could find fresh food
for himself.

Caleb had come to love the little donkey. He was frisky, kicking up his heels at the slightest noise and braying with alarm if a branch fell from the trees around him. Caleb liked the donkey's big, wide eyes and soft mouth. Caleb wondered, though, if the colt would ever be tamed!

Caleb's father wondered, too. He had never owned such a nervous colt. It was time to begin hiring him out to visitors in Jerusalem. But first he had to be broken. Caleb's father sighed. He felt he was getting too old to "break in" any more donkeys, and he wasn't sure Caleb was old enough.

As if reading his father's thoughts, Caleb said, "Let me try to ride him, Father, please. He knows me and perhaps he'll let me sit on him."

"Why not?" replied Caleb's father with a twinkle in his eye. Caleb could only fall onto the soft grass and no harm would be done.

The colt eyed Caleb and his father suspiciously. But after a while, he allowed the pair to touch him and even place a rope around his neck to act as a rough halter.

Caleb jumped onto the colt's back but the colt reared up and threw the boy right over his head.

Luckily, Caleb landed right in the middle of a pile of vine branches!

"He's not ready to let anyone ride him, that's for sure," Caleb's father chuckled as he helped Caleb onto his feet.

Suddenly two men appeared. Caleb recognized them as two of his father's friends, Peter and John. They had been helping Jesus, the teacher from Galilee. Caleb had heard about Jesus. He helped the sick get well. Many even said He raised people from the dead!

Peter and John greeted Caleb's father, and then told him they needed to borrow the colt.

"Our Master, Jesus, has need of him," they said.

"Why?" asked Caleb in surprise.

"He needs a donkey to ride into Jerusalem tomorrow," replied Peter.

"Well, He doesn't need this one!" exclaimed Caleb, rubbing a big bump that appeared on the side of his head.

"Oh, but He does," said John. "He sent us to bring this very colt. Don't worry. Jesus will know what to do with him!" John added, smiling at the boy.

"Go with the colt, Caleb," his father said. "Do whatever needs to be done for Jesus!"

Caleb's heart began to beat furiously. He was going to meet Jesus, the man who made blind men see, dumb men speak, and deaf men hear!

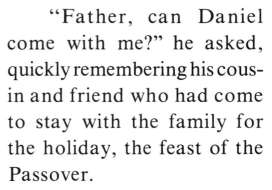

"Father, can Daniel come with me?" he asked, quickly remembering his cousin and friend who had come to stay with the family for the holiday, the feast of the Passover.

Daniel lived in the little village of Emmaus. When he was not in school, he helped his father and mother keep the inn in the village.

Caleb's father smiled. "If Daniel wants to go with you, he can," he replied.

Caleb untied the colt from the donkey stake and set off down the road, tugging the donkey after him. At first, the little colt refused to move at all. But eventually, he began to follow Caleb, kicking up his heels at the slightest sound and braying loudly, showing his bright, white teeth in a naughty smile that seemed to say, "I'll come along with you, Caleb, but don't think I'm going to be good!"

Caleb led the colt to his house and called Daniel to come and join him. Daniel ran down the stone steps into the courtyard and laughed when he saw Caleb pulling and pushing the reluctant donkey.

"Why, that's the stubbornest donkey I've ever seen," Daniel said.

"Jesus wants him," puffed Caleb, "though I can't imagine why! Come on, we have to take the colt to the Mount of Olives."

The two boys set off with the colt. Once inside the city gates, in the midst of the noisy traffic in the busy streets of Jerusalem, the colt became terrified. It took all Daniel's and Caleb's strength to hold onto the rope.

"Why did we come this way?" panted Daniel, helping Caleb hang onto the colt's halter and steer him in the right direction.

"It's quicker," answered Caleb.

The colt bumped into a man carrying bread on his head. The loaves rolled all over the ground. The donkey then frightened some little boys when he kicked up his heels at their shouts. After that, he took off at a terrific pace, dragging Caleb and Daniel behind him. By the time they arrived at the Mount of Olives, the boys were hot and dirty and very glad to hand the colt over to someone else!

It was easy to find Jesus. There was a crowd of people around Him.

"There's Jesus!" shouted Caleb excitedly.

The boys saw a man with the most kindly smile they had ever seen. They knew at once that Jesus was in charge! He looked like a king, even though His clothes were the clothes of a poor man.

"Thank you, Caleb and Daniel," said Jesus. "Thank you for bringing the colt."

"Sir," gulped Caleb, wondering how Jesus knew their names, "I don't think You should ride him. You might be in trouble!"

Jesus laughed and everyone around joined in. You couldn't help it! The boys felt their very hearts smiling inside them at the sound of His laughter!

Taking the rough halter in His hand, Jesus looked at the little colt with great kindness. The wide, frightened eyes of the animal seemed to smile back as if to say, "I wouldn't do this for anyone else in the whole world!"

Caleb and Daniel saw Jesus mount the donkey and set off down the hill toward Jerusalem. The crowd began tearing branches off the trees, throwing them under the little colt's feet. Someone began to shout "Hosanna! Blessed be He that comes in the name of the Lord!" Others took up the cry until the sound filled the air. Daniel and Caleb set off after Jesus and the donkey, unable to believe their eyes. The colt was behaving perfectly, picking his way over the palm branches and holding his little head up proudly as if to say, "This is the most important day of my life!"

Daniel and Caleb caught up with Jesus and proudly led the donkey along. Why, all Jerusalem seemed to be there! They came to a halt. Jesus dismounted and turned the colt over to Caleb and Daniel.

"Now you two can ride him home," Jesus said. "He won't throw you over his head this time, Caleb."

Wondering how Jesus knew that the colt had thrown him the first time, Caleb took the animal from Jesus's hands.

"I've never seen a colt ridden before he was broken," Daniel said very timidly to Jesus.

"He knows Me," Jesus replied. "I made him," He added. Then Jesus was gone, leaving Caleb and Daniel gazing after Him.

"What did He mean?" Caleb asked Daniel.

"I don't know," replied Daniel.

"But only God can make a donkey," sputtered Caleb.

"I know," Daniel said very quietly.

As the two boys rode home, they were amazed at the colt's obedience. They rushed into Caleb's home to tell his parents about the colt letting Jesus sit on him. Caleb's father seemed to be far more worried about what the Jewish leaders thought about the people calling Jesus a king and welcoming Him into Jerusalem.

"The Jews won't like this," Caleb's father said to himself, "nor will the Romans. I'm afraid Jesus will be in trouble."

A few days later, Daniel and Caleb heard some bad news from their friend Simon who lived next door. "Jesus has been arrested," he told them.

"Why?" asked the boys in astonishment.

"No one can find out," said Simon in a low voice.

"Perhaps we can," said Caleb, hoisting a batch of fresh bread onto his shoulder. The boys were to deliver the bread to the fortress where the Governor's soldiers were guarding Jesus.

Inside the Roman fortress the boys found a servant girl who was happy to tell them all she knew. She had been sweeping the courtyard when the soldiers brought Jesus in.

"Two of His friends were with Him," she reported.

"Oh, that's good," sighed Caleb with relief. "Peter and John must have been with Him."

"Some friends they turned out to be," continued the girl. "They said they didn't know Him."

Caleb and Daniel looked at each other in horror.

"I don't blame them, mind you," continued the girl. "The Governor, Pontius Pilate, had Jesus whipped. Perhaps His friends were afraid they would be whipped, too."

The two boys ran home to tell Caleb's father what had

happened. The older man looked very upset when he heard the boys' report.

"If they have taken Jesus to the Governor," he said, "they probably intend to ask for the death sentence."

"But what has He done?" asked Caleb, angry at the soldiers for arresting Jesus.

"Some of the Jewish and Roman leaders hate Jesus because He has been saying He is God," replied Caleb's father.

"Only God can make donkeys," murmured Daniel.

"Father," asked Caleb, "do you think He is God?"

"Yes, my son, I do," replied Caleb's father.

There was a long silence in the room after that—each quiet with his own thoughts.

The boys slept lightly that night, tossing and turning in their beds. They awoke early in the morning and their first thoughts were about Jesus.

Caleb's father sent them on errands most of the morning. The boys ran down the colorful, narrow streets that wound in and out of the ancient stone buildings. The streets were busier than usual because Jerusalem was filled with visitors for the Passover.

Suddenly, a huge crowd blocked the way ahead of them. There were angry shouts and the sounds of women crying. The two boys found themselves squashed tightly together against the wall. They couldn't see anything and could only guess what was going on around them.

After the commotion was over, the boys ran to a shop and asked what it was all about.

"The Romans were taking three men to be crucified," the shopkeeper announced. "One of them was that carpenter everyone is talking about, Jesus of Nazareth."

"We've got to stop them!" Caleb cried.

"And how are two boys like you going to do that?" inquired the shopkeeper good-humoredly. "Perhaps you intend to take on the might of Rome all by yourselves?"

"But, but," sputtered Daniel, "He's God! They mustn't be allowed to kill God!"

"Well now, if Jesus really is God, I don't think He will allow the soldiers to kill Him, do you?" asked the shopkeeper.

"I don't suppose so," muttered Caleb. He was confused and very, very frightened.

The two boys raced home through the streets which were filled once more with busy sounds of buying and selling.

When they arrived, Caleb's father was talking to a neighbor.

"Father! They are going to kill Jesus!" shouted Caleb.

Caleb's father turned toward them, his face the saddest Caleb had ever seen it.

"I know, my son. This is a terrible day."

All at once, the sky became dark as night, even though it was only noon.

"Even the sun hides its face from us," Daniel whispered in the smallest of voices.

The colt that had carried Jesus into Jerusalem was standing near the wall of the courtyard, swishing his tail around this way and that and tossing his head. His eyes became wide and wild.

"The colt knows about Jesus," said Daniel. "Look at him!"

Suddenly the whole earth began to shake.

"God have mercy upon us!" shouted Caleb's father. "God is judging us!"

Throwing their arms around the children, the men in the courtyard fell to their knees in fear. As quickly as it had begun, the quaking ground ceased to rumble and roar and an unearthly stillness settled around them.

The donkey was making little troubled noises and Caleb ran to him, putting his arms around the colt's warm neck and seeking to comfort him.

"Jesus is dead," exclaimed Caleb, "how could anyone kill Him? He was so kind."

"Maybe He will not stay dead!" interrupted Daniel. "If He really is God, maybe He will come back from the grave and deliver us from the Romans."

"Who knows, Daniel," replied Caleb's father with tears in his eyes. "Who knows what will happen now!"

Three days passed and Caleb's father felt that his son

should go away for a few days to forget the events of the past week. He decided to send Caleb home with Daniel. Emmaus, where Daniel lived, was a quiet little village. It would do Caleb good to get out into the countryside. Caleb loved to help at the inn, serving the guests and making himself useful.

Safely in Emmaus, Daniel and Caleb shared the events of the last few days with Daniel's family.

"Who knows?" said Daniel's mother. "If indeed Jesus is God, then He will come back to us and set His people free."

"He told us He made the colt," Caleb said.

"And only God can make a donkey," added Daniel.

All day the children helped Daniel's father clean and prepare the food for the evening meal. Late that night, just as it was time to bolt the door, three strangers came to the door of the inn.

"It's late," grumbled Daniel's father. "Who are these people who come at such a time expecting food and lodging?"

"But it's dark," Daniel's mother reminded him. "We must take them in. It's too late for them to go on to the next village. There are robbers about and the roads are dangerous."

"Yes, you're right," replied Daniel's father. "Daniel! Caleb! Come quickly! Set the table with good food. Make sure the guests are comfortable."

Daniel and Caleb ran into the inn and found the three guests sitting at the table talking earnestly together. Suddenly Daniel heard a braying in the courtyard.

"Run outside, Caleb," he said, "the man's donkey will need food and water."

Caleb ran outside and right into his colt!

"What are you doing here?" he said to the donkey in astonishment.

Whirling around, he raced back into the kitchen. "Aunt! Uncle!" he called, "my colt! The one Jesus rode into Jerusalem! He's here!"

"Well, what of it?" asked Daniel's father. "The colt was probably hired from your father for one of the visitors to Jerusalem."

"But . . . my father told me he would never hire that colt out again—not after Jesus had ridden him into Jerusalem that day."

Daniel's father stared at Caleb.

"Maybe your father changed his mind," he said.

Before Caleb could reply, Daniel ran into the kitchen.

"He's—He's gone!" he stuttered.

"Who's gone?" asked his father.

"The Man, one of the three men who have just come!"

"Without paying?" asked Daniel's mother.

"I saw His hands when He broke the bread," said Daniel, his voice wavering. "They—they had holes in the palms."

"Jesus!" shouted Caleb.

"Yes!" answered Daniel, his face shining. "Jesus! Then He vanished!"

"But the door was locked! I locked it," said Daniel's father.

"The God who made donkeys has no trouble with locked doors!" laughed Daniel.

The family hurried into the dining room. The two men were standing with their arms around each other and they were crying with joy. "Didn't our hearts leap when He talked with us?" said one to the other.

"God has visited His people," said Daniel's father in awe. "He came, I think, to do more than deliver us from the Romans. He came to deliver us from the fear of death."

Caleb ran outside to feed and water his colt. The animal

had the loveliest light in his eyes. He looked so content, as if he had just had a loving pat on his funny little head and enjoyed someone's tender, strong fingers playing with his rough mane. He looked for all the world as if he was smiling.

"Maybe he is," said Caleb to himself. "Perhaps Jesus passed by!"

The colt brayed as if to say, "He did, Caleb. He did and He told me He won't be needing me anymore. He's going home!"